WILDLIFE VIEWING AREAS

Indiana Ecoregions

- Southern Michigan/Northern Indiana Drift Plains
- Interior River Valleys and Hills
- Eastern Corn Belt Plains
- Central Corn Belt Plains
- Huron/Erie Lake Plains
- Interior Plateau

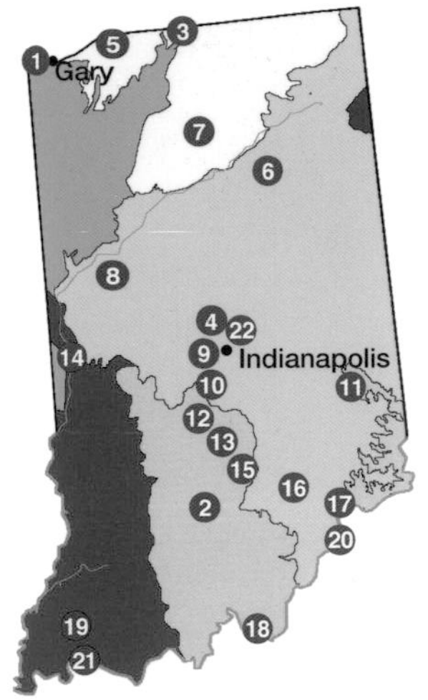

1. Hammond Lakefront Park & Bird Sanctuary
2. Spring Mill State Park
3. Rum Village Nature Center
4. Fort Harrison State Park
5. Indiana Dunes State Park Nature Center
6. Salamonie River State Forest/Reservoir
7. Potawatomi Wildlife Park
8. Celery Bog Nature Area/Lilly Nature Center
9. Eagle Creek Park/ Bird Sanctuary
10. Indianapolis Zoo
11. Mary Gray Bird Sanctuary
12. Morgan-Monroe State Forest/Scout Ridge Nature Preserve
13. Brown County State Park Nature Center
14. Turkey Run State Park
15. Charles C. Deam Wilderness
16. Muscatatuck National Wildlife Refuge
17. Big Oaks NWR
18. O'Bannon Woods Interpretive Center
19. Patoka River NWR
20. Cllfty Falls State Park
21. Lincoln State Park Nature Center
22. Holliday Park & Nature Center

Most illustrations show the adult male in breeding coloration. Colors and markings may be duller or absent during different seasons. The measurements denote the length of animals from nose/bill to tail tip. Butterfly measurements denote wingspan. Illustrations are not to scale.

Waterford Press produces reference guides that introduce novices to nature, science, travel and languages. Product information is featured on the website: **www.waterfordpress.com**

To order, call 800-434-2555. For permissions, or to share comments, e-mail editor@waterfordpress.com. For information on custom-published products, call 800-434-2555 or e-mail info@waterfordpress.com.

Scan for more info

Made in the USA

ISBN 978-1-58355-476-0
$7.95 U.S.
9 781583 554760 50795
UPC 8 84682 01002 7
10 9 8 7 6 5 4 3 2
709223

INDIANA WILDLIFE – A Folding Pocket Guide to Familiar Animals

Kavanagh/Leung

A POCKET NATURALIST® GUIDE

INDIANA WILDLIFE

A Folding Pocket Guide to Familiar Animals

BUTTERFLIES

Spicebush Swallowtail
Papilio troilus
To 4.5 in. (11 cm)

Black Swallowtail
Papilio polyxenes
To 3.5 in. (9 cm)

Eastern Tiger Swallowtail
Papilio glaucus
To 6 in. (15 cm)

Eastern Tailed Blue
Everes comyntas
To 1 in. (3 cm)

Little Yellow
Eurema lisa
To 1.5 in. (4 cm)

Cabbage White
Pieris rapae
To 2 in. (5 cm)

American Copper
Lycaena phlaeas
To 1.25 in. (3.2 cm)

Red-spotted Purple
Limenitis arthemis astyanax
To 3.5 in. (9 cm)

Summer Azure
Celastrina neglecta
To 1 in. (3 cm)

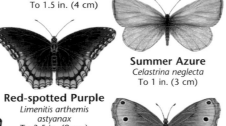

Monarch
Danaus plexippus
To 4 in. (10 cm)

Comma
Polygonia comma
To 2 in. (5 cm)
Has a silvery comma mark on the underside of its hindwings.

Little Wood Satyr
Megisto cymela
To 2 in. (5 cm)

Great Spangled Fritillary
Speyeria cybele
To 3 in. (8 cm)

Mourning Cloak
Nymphalis antiopa
To 3.5 in. (9 cm)

White Admiral
Limenitis arthemis arthemis
To 3 in. (8 cm)

Underwings
Silver-spotted Skipper
Epargyreus clarus
To 2.5 in. (6 cm)
Has a large, irregular silver patch on the underside of its hindwings.

Viceroy
Limenitis archippus
To 3 in. (8 cm)
Told from similar monarch by its smaller size and the thin, black band on its hindwings.

INSECTS

German Cockroach
Blatella germanica
To .5 in. (1.3 cm)
Note 2 dark stripes on upper part of thorax. Can climb slick surfaces like glass.

House Cricket
Acheta domestica
To 1 in. (3 cm)
Note long antennae and long hind legs.

Differential Grasshopper
Melanoplus femur-rubrum
To 1.75 in. (4.5 cm)

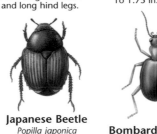

Eastern Toe-biter
Benacus griseus
To 2.5 in. (6.5 cm)

Japanese Beetle
Popilla japonica
To .5 in. (1.5 cm)
Common garden pest.

Bombardier Beetle
Brachinus spp.
To .5 in. (1.3 cm)
Emits an explosive toxic substance from its anal glands when disturbed.

Ladybug Beetle
Family Coccinellidae
To .5 in. (1.3 cm)
Red wing covers are black-spotted.

Aphid
Family Aphididae
To .5 in. (1.3 cm)
Pear-shaped, soft bodied insect feeds on the sap of plants. Color varies from red and green to black.

Say's Firefly
Pyractomena angulata
To .5 in. (1.4 cm)

Green Lacewings
Family Chrysopidae
To .75 in. (2 cm)
Clear wings have green veins.

Honey Bee
Apis mellifera
To .75 in. (2 cm)
Slender bee has pollen baskets on its rear legs.

Mosquito
Family Culicidae
To .5 in. (1.3 cm)
Slender insect has a thin, blood-sucking beak.

American House Spider
Achaearanea tepidariorum
To .25 in. (.6 cm)
Has bulbous, yellow-brown abdomen. Common indoors.

Green Stink Bug
Acrosternum hilare
To .75 in. (1.9 cm)

♀
Black-and-yellow Argiope
Argiope aurantia
To 1.25 in. (3.2 cm)

Black Carpenter Ant
Camponotus pennsylvanicus
To .5 in. (1.2 cm)

American Bumble Bee
Bombus pennsylvanicus
To 1 in. (2.5 cm)

FISHES

Northern Pike
Esox lucius To 53 in. (1.4 m)
Note large head and posterior dorsal fin.

Muskellunge
Esox masquinongy To 6 ft. (1.8 m)
Prized sport fish is an aggressive predator.

Channel Catfish
Ictalurus punctatus To 4 ft. (1.2 m)
Note prominent 'whiskers'.

Redear Sunfish
Lepomis microlophus To 14 in. (35 cm)
Has orange or red spot near dark ear flap. Also called shellcracker.

Bluegill
Lepomis macrochirus
To 16 in. (40 cm)

Black Crappie
Pomoxis nigromaculatus
To 16 in. (40 cm)
Note humped back.

Smallmouth Bass
Micropterus dolomieu To 27 in. (68 cm)
Jaw joint is beneath the eye.

Striped Bass
Morone saxatilis To 6 ft. (1.8 m)
Has 6-9 dark side stripes.

Largemouth Bass
Micropterus salmoides To 40 in. (1 m)
Jaw joint extends beyond the eye.

Coho (Silver) Salmon
Oncorhynchus kisutch To 40 in. (1 m)
Has white gums and a black tongue. Breeding male has red side stripes.

Rainbow Trout
Oncorhynchus mykiss To 44 in. (1.1 m)
Has pink to red side stripe.

Lake Trout
Salvelinus namaycush To 4 ft. (1.2 m)
Dark fish is covered in light spots. Tail is deeply forked.

Brown Trout
Salmo trutta To 40 in. (1 m)
Has red and black spots on its body.

Walleye
Sander vitreus To 40 in. (1 m)
Note white spot on lower lobe of tail.

REPTILES & AMPHIBIANS

Snapping Turtle
Chelydra serpentina To 18 in. (45 cm)
Note knobby shell and long tail.

Midland Painted Turtle
Chrysemys picta marginata
To 10 in. (25 cm)

Map Turtle
Graptemys geographica
To 11 in. (28 cm)
Note yellow spot behind eye.

Eastern Box Turtle
Terrapene carolina To 9 in. (23 cm)
Note high-domed shell.

Eastern Hognose Snake
Heterodon platyrhinos To 4 ft. (1.2 m)
Thick snake has an upturned snout. Color varies from jet black to yellowish.

Five-lined Skink
Plestidon fasciatus To 8 in. (20 cm)
Has 5 light dorsal stripes.

Midland Brown Snake
Storeria dekayi wrightorum
To 20 in. (50 cm)
Has 2 rows of dark spots down its back.

Common Garter Snake
Thamnophis sirtalis To 4 ft. (1.2 m)
Slender snake has has three yellowish stripes. Coloration is highly variable.

Blue Racer
Coluber constrictor foxii To 6.5 ft. (2 m)

Black Rat Snake
Elaphe obsoleta obsoleta
To 8 ft. (2.4 m)

Mudpuppy
Necturus maculosus To 16 in. (40 cm)
Told by feathery, reddish external gills.

Green Frog
lithobates clamitans melanota
To 4 in. (10 cm)
Single-note call is a banjo-like twang.

Tiger Salamander
Ambystoma tigrinum tigrinum
To 13 in. (33 cm)

Blanchard's Cricket Frog
Acris crepitans blanchardii
To 1.5 in. (4 cm)
Call is a measured clicking. Diurnal.

Woodhouse's Toad
Anaxyrus woodhousei
To 5 in. (13 cm)
Call is a sheep-like bleating.

Bullfrog
Lithobates catesbeianus
To 8 in. (20 cm)
Call is a deep-pitched – *jug-o-rum*.

BIRDS

Mallard
Anas platyrhynchos
To 28 in. (70 cm)

Blue-winged Teal
Anas discors
To 16 in. (40 cm)

Wood Duck
Aix sponsa To 20 in. (50 cm)

American Black Duck
Anas rubripes
To 25 in. (63 cm)
Note yellow bill.

Pied-billed Grebe
Podilymbus podiceps
To 13 in. (33 cm)
Note banded white bill.

Great Blue Heron
Ardea herodias
To 4.5 ft. (1.4 m)

Canada Goose
Branta canadensis
To 45 in. (1.14 m)

Ring-billed Gull
Larus delawarensis
To 20 in. (50 cm)
Bill has dark ring.

Bald Eagle
Haliaeetus leucocephalus
To 40 in. (1 m)

Green Heron
Butorides virescens
To 22 in. (55 cm)

Killdeer
Charadrius vociferus
To 12 in. (30 cm)
Note two breast bands.

Cooper's Hawk
Accipiter cooperii
To 20 in. (50 cm)
Note long, rounded white-tipped tail. Often found in urban areas.

Red-tailed Hawk
Buteo jamaicensis
To 25 in. (63 cm)

Northern Harrier
Circus cyaneus
To 22 in. (55 cm)
Note V-shaped flight profile and white rump.

BIRDS

Turkey Vulture
Cathartes aura
To 32 in. (80 cm)
Note red head and two-toned underwings.

Red-shouldered Hawk
Buteo lineatus
To 22 in. (55 cm)

American Kestrel
Falco sparverius
To 12 in. (30 cm)

Great Horned Owl
Bubo virginianus
To 25 in. (63 cm)
Call is a resonant –
hoo-HOO-hoooo.

Wild Turkey
Meleagris gallopavo
To 4 ft. (1.2 m)

Barred Owl
Strix varia
To 2 ft. (60 cm)
Call is a loud –
who-cooks-for-you?
who-cooks-for-you-all?

Rock Pigeon
Columba livia
To 13 in. (33 cm)

Belted Kingfisher
Megaceryle alcyon
To 14 in. (35 cm)

Mourning Dove
Zenaida macroura
To 13 in. (33 cm)
Call is a mournful –
ooah-woo-woo-woo.

Ruby-throated Hummingbird
Archilochus colubris
To 3.5 in. (9 cm)

Northern Bobwhite
Colinus virginianus
To 12 in. (30 cm)

Northern Flicker
Colaptes auratus
To 13 in. (33 cm)
Wing and tail linings are yellow.

Pileated Woodpecker
Dryocopus pileatus
To 17 in. (43 cm)
Note large size.

Red-bellied Woodpecker
Melanerpes carolinus
To 11 in. (28 cm)

Downy Woodpecker
Picoides pubescens
To 6 in. (15 cm)
The similar hairy woodpecker is larger and has a longer bill.

BIRDS

Great Crested Flycatcher
Myiarchus crinitus
To 9 in. (23 cm)

Eastern Kingbird
Tyrannus tyrannus
To 8 in. (20 cm)
Note broad white tail band.

Blue Jay
Cyanocitta cristata
To 14 in. (35 cm)

Red-eyed Vireo
Vireo olivaceus
To 6 in. (15 cm)

Tree Swallow
Tachycineta bicolor
To 6 in. (15 cm)

American Crow
Corvus brachyrhynchos
To 22 in. (55 cm)
Call is a distinct – caw.

Northern Mockingbird
Mimus polyglottos
To 11 in. (28 cm)

White-breasted Nuthatch
Sitta carolinensis
To 6 in. (15 cm)

Carolina Wren
Thryothorus ludovicianus
To 6 in. (15 cm)

Tufted Titmouse
Baeolophus bicolor
To 6 in. (15 cm)

Horned Lark
Eremophila alpestris
To 8 in. (20 cm)

Eastern Bluebird
Sialia sialis
To 7 in. (18 cm)

European Starling
Sturnus vulgaris
To 8 in. (20 cm)

American Robin
Turdus migratorius
To 11 in. (28 cm)

Brown Thrasher
Toxostoma rufum
To 12 in. (30 cm)

BIRDS

Yellow Warbler
Setophaga petechia
To 5 in. (13 cm)

Scarlet Tanager
Piranga olivacea
To 7 in. (18 cm)

Cedar Waxwing
Bombycilla cedrorum
To 7 in. (18 cm)
Red wing marks look like waxy droplets.

Common Yellowthroat
Geothlypis trichas
To 5 in. (13 cm)

Red-winged Blackbird
Agelaius phoeniceus
To 9 in. (23 cm)

Common Grackle
Quiscalus quiscula
To 14 in. (35 cm)

Eastern Meadowlark
Sturnella magna
To 9 in. (23 cm)

Indigo Bunting
Passerina cyanea
To 6 in. (15 cm)

Brown-headed Cowbird
Molothrus ater
To 7 in. (18 cm)

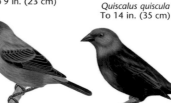
Song Sparrow
Melospiza melodia
To 7 in. (18 cm)
Note central breast spot.

Baltimore Oriole
Icterus galbula
To 8 in. (20 cm)

American Goldfinch
Spinus tristis
To 5 in. (13 cm)

House Sparrow
Passer domesticus
To 6 in. (15 cm)

Northern Cardinal
Cardinalis cardinalis
To 9 in. (23 cm)
Indiana's state bird.

House Finch
Haemorhous mexicanus
To 6 in. (15 cm)

MAMMALS

Virginia Opossum
Didelphis virginiana
To 40 in. (1 m)
Note long fur and naked tail.

Hoary Bat
Lasiurus cinereus
To 6 in. (15 cm)
Brown fur is white-tipped.

Big Brown Bat
Eptesicus fuscus
To 5 in. (13 cm)

Eastern Cottontail
Sylvilagus floridanus
To 18 in. (45 cm)

Southern Flying Squirrel
Glaucomys volans
To 10 in. (25 cm)

European Rabbit
Oryctolagus cuniculus
To 2 ft. (60 cm)

Eastern Chipmunk
Tamias striatus
To 12 in. (30 cm)
Note white stripes on side and face.

Fox Squirrel
Sciurus niger To 28 in. (70 cm)
Note large size and bushy tail. Largest squirrel in US.

Eastern Gray Squirrel
Sciurus carolinensis
To 20 in. (50 cm)

Deer Mouse
Peromyscus maniculatus
To 8 in. (20 cm)
Distinguished by white undersides and hairy tail.

Norway Rat
Rattus norvegicus
To 18 in. (45 cm)
Brown to gray rodent has a naked tail.

House Mouse
Mus musculus To 8 in. (20 cm)
Introduced pest has a naked tail.

Woodchuck
Marmota monax
To 32 in. (80 cm)

Meadow Vole
Microtus pennsylvanicus
To 7 in. (18 cm)
Small mouse-like creature has long fur and a short tail.

Franklin's Ground Squirrel
Poliocitellus franklinii
To 16 in. (40 cm)
Call is a bird-like whistling.

MAMMALS

American Beaver
Castor canadensis
To 4 ft. (1.2 m)

Common Muskrat
Ondatra zibethicus
To 2 ft. (60 cm)
Aquatic rodent has a naked, scaly tail.

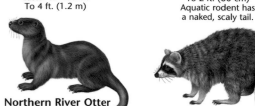
Northern River Otter
Lontra canadensis
To 52 in. (1.3 m)

Common Raccoon
Procyon lotor
To 40 in. (1 m)

Long-tailed Weasel
Mustela frenata To 21 in. (53 cm)
Note brown feet and yellowish neck.

Striped Skunk
Mephitis mephitis
To 32 in. (80 cm)

American Badger
Taxidea taxus
To 35 in. (88 cm)

Bobcat
Lynx rufus
To 4 ft. (1.2 m)

Common Gray Fox
Urocyon cinereoargenteus
To 3.5 ft. (1.1 m)
Note black-tipped tail.

Red Fox
Vulpes vulpes To 40 in. (1 m)
Note white-tipped tail.

White-tailed Deer
Odocoileus virginianus
To 7 ft. (2.1 m)
Fluffy tail is white below and held aloft when running.

Coyote
Canis latrans To 52 in. (1.3 m)
Note bushy, black-tipped tail.

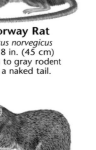